AND SPACE
SCIENCE

GLOBAL CLIMATE
CHANGE

By Christina Earley

A Stingray Book

SEAHORSE
PUBLISHING

Teaching Tips for Caregivers and Teachers:

This Hi-Lo book features high-interest subject matter that will appeal to all readers in intermediate and middle school grades. It may be enjoyed by students reading at or above grade level as well as by those who are looking for age-appropriate themes matched with a less challenging reading level. Hi-Lo books are ideal for ELL readers, too.

Each book appeals to a striving reader's age and maturity level. Opportunities are provided for students to read words they already know while encountering a limited number of new, high-interest vocabulary words. With these supports in place, students will read more fluently while increasing reading comprehension. Use the following suggestions to help students grow as readers.

- Encourage the student to read independently at home.
- Encourage the student to practice reading aloud.
- Encourage activities that require reading.
- Establish a regular reading time.
- Have the student write questions about what they read.

Teaching Tips for Teachers:

Before Reading

- Ask, "What do I know about this topic?"
- Ask, "What do I want to learn about this topic?"

During Reading

- Ask, "What is the author trying to teach me?"
- Ask, "How is this like something I already know?"

After Reading

- Discuss how the text features (headings, index, etc.) help with understanding the topic.
- Ask, "What interesting or fun fact did you learn?"

TABLE OF CONTENTS

CLIMATE CHANGE 4

WEATHER vs. CLIMATE. 6

A WARMING EARTH 8

CARBON. 10

CHANGES OVER TIME 12

IMPACTS TO EARTH 14

MONITORING CHANGE 16

CAREER: PALEOCLIMATOLOGIST. 18

INVESTIGATE: THE GREENHOUSE EFFECT 20

THE SCIENTIFIC METHOD .21

SCIENTIST SPOTLIGHT 21

GLOSSARY 22

INDEX 23

AFTER READING QUESTIONS. 23

ABOUT THE AUTHOR 24

CLIMATE CHANGE

Climate change is a change in the usual weather for an area over a long period of time.

Scientists have observed that Earth is warming.

This is causing rising sea levels, shrinking **glaciers**, and changes to the times when plants grow.

Earth's average temperature has been increasing more quickly than expected over the past 150 years.

When glaciers melt, sea levels rise.

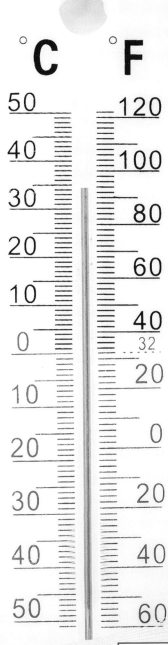

FUN FACTS

Many of the warmest years on record have happened in the past 20 years.

WEATHER VS. CLIMATE

Weather is the condition of the **atmosphere** over a short time. It can change in a few hours.

Climate is the typical weather conditions in a region for at least 30 years. It includes the average high and low temperatures that are expected in an area.

Satellite sensors map global temperatures.

FUN FACTS

Weather includes temperature, wind, cloudiness, humidity, precipitation, and atmospheric pressure.

A WARMING EARTH

Carbon dioxide and other gases collect in Earth's atmosphere. They trap the Sun's heat.

This is like the way a greenhouse's glass walls and roof keep heat inside.

Human activities, such as burning trees and **fossil fuels**, put more carbon dioxide into the air.

More of the Sun's heat is trapped. The planet warms up.

THE GREENHOUSE EFFECT

energy released back into space

greenhouse gases trap heat

energy absorbed

FUN FACTS

Earth's atmosphere is 78 percent nitrogen, 21 percent oxygen, 0.9 percent argon, and 0.1 percent carbon dioxide and other gases.

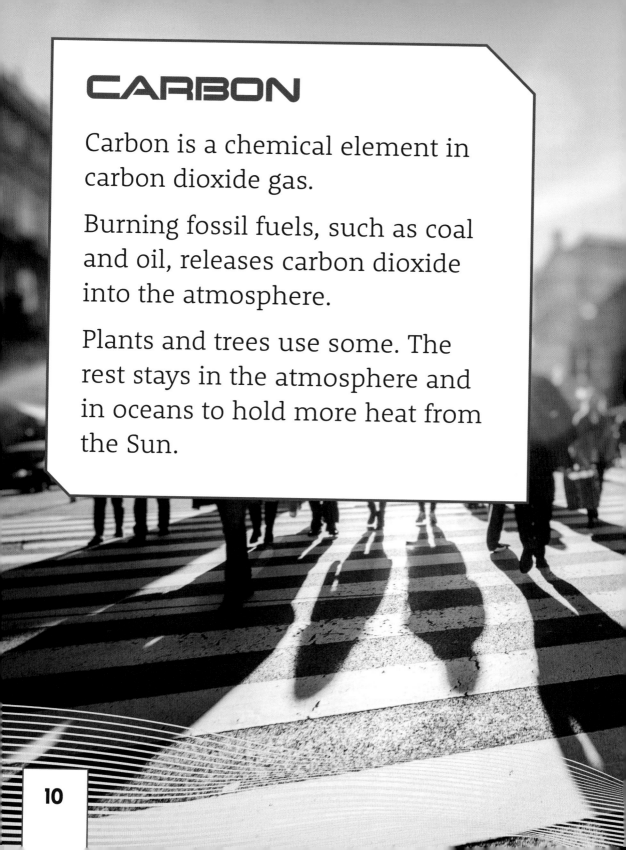

CARBON

Carbon is a chemical element in carbon dioxide gas.

Burning fossil fuels, such as coal and oil, releases carbon dioxide into the atmosphere.

Plants and trees use some. The rest stays in the atmosphere and in oceans to hold more heat from the Sun.

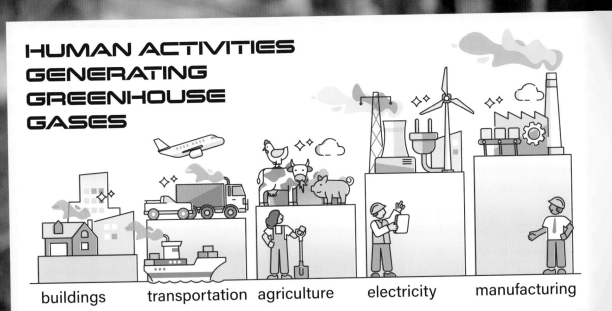

HUMAN ACTIVITIES GENERATING GREENHOUSE GASES

buildings   transportation   agriculture   electricity   manufacturing

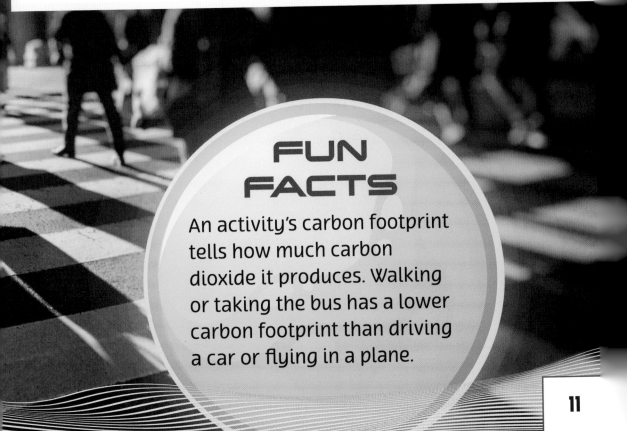

FUN FACTS

An activity's carbon footprint tells how much carbon dioxide it produces. Walking or taking the bus has a lower carbon footprint than driving a car or flying in a plane.

CHANGES OVER TIME

Earth's climate has warmed and cooled many times over history.

When the Sun's engine is more active, temperatures can rise.

Now, the Sun is less active. But Earth is still warming.

Average global air temperatures have gone up about two degrees Fahrenheit (one degree Celsius) in the last 100 years.

The last ice age ended about 12,000 years ago.

FUN FACTS

There have been
cycles of ice age
warmer periods
last 800,000 ye

IMPACTS TO EARTH

A few degrees of temperature change make a big difference to Earth's plants and animals.

High temperatures make it hard for crops to grow.

The cold **habitat** that polar bears and penguins need is melting away.

Acidity caused by extra carbon dioxide in the ocean is damaging coral reefs. Many sea creatures depend on this habitat. Ocean food webs are disrupted.

FUN FACTS

Scientists predict the Arctic could be free of summer ice as soon as 2040.

MONITORING CHANGE

Scientists use many tools on the ground, in the ocean, and in space to study Earth's climate.

Computer programs help scientists analyze air bubbles found in glacial ice.

Robotic Argo floats record the temperatures and salt levels of oceans.

Satellites measure carbon dioxide in the atmosphere.

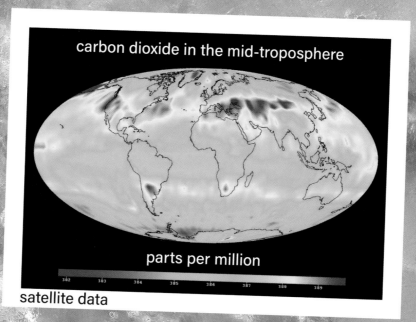

carbon dioxide in the mid-troposphere

parts per million

satellite data

Argo float

CAREER: PALEOCLIMATOLOGIST

Paleoclimatologists use data to understand Earth's climate at different times in history.

Their research has been credited with explaining the **greenhouse effect**.

These scientists examine tree rings, ice cores, and animal remains to learn what Earth's atmosphere was like in the past.

They work in labs, but they also collect samples from the areas they are investigating.

INVESTIGATE: THE GREENHOUSE EFFECT

Materials:

- 5 glass mason jars
- Masking tape
- Permanent marker
- White vinegar
- Baking soda
- Measuring cups and spoons
- Plastic wrap
- Rubber bands
- A heat source such as a sunny window, heat lamp, or space heater
- Thermometer
- Scissors
- Paper and pencil

Procedure:

(1) Use the tape and marker to label the jars: *Air, Vinegar, Baking Soda, Reaction 1,* and *Reaction 2.*

(2) Leave the *Air* jar empty. Pour one-quarter cup vinegar into the *Vinegar* jar. Put one tablespoon baking soda into the *Baking Soda* jar. Cover each jar with plastic wrap and secure with a rubber band. These jars are the controls in your experiment.

(3) Put one tablespoon baking soda into the *Reaction 1* jar. Add one-quarter cup vinegar. The reaction will release carbon dioxide gas. Quickly cover with plastic wrap and secure with a rubber band. Ask another person to help so that you capture all the gas. This jar represents the greenhouse effect.

(4) Place the first four jars in front of the heat source. Make sure all are positioned to heat evenly.

(5) Put one tablespoon baking soda into the *Reaction 2* jar. Add one-quarter cup vinegar. Do not cover or heat this jar. After 30 seconds, use the thermometer to take a temperature reading of the air in the jar. Make a note.

(6) After 10 minutes, take the temperature of the air in each heated jar. Cut a slit in the plastic wrap just large enough to slide in the thermometer. After one minute, remove the thermometer and read the temperature. Make a note.

(7) Draw conclusions from your data. What was the effect of the heat source?

THE SCIENTIFIC METHOD

- Ask a question.
- Gather information and observe.
- Make a hypothesis or guess the answer.
- Experiment and test your hypothesis, or guess.
- Analyze your test results.
- Modify your hypothesis, if necessary.
- Make a conclusion.

SCIENTIST SPOTLIGHT

Eunice Newton Foote was an American scientist, inventor, and campaigner for women's rights. In 1856, she conducted the first scientific research to demonstrate the existence of greenhouse gases. After testing many gases, she discovered that carbon dioxide traps heat from sunlight. She concluded that there is a connection between air temperature and the concentration of carbon dioxide in the atmosphere.

GLOSSARY

acidity (uh-SID-i-tee): the amount of acid that a substance contains; an acid is a chemical compound that reacts with a base to form a salt, that has a pH lower than 7, and that can cause burning and other damage

atmosphere (AT-muhs-feer): the mixture of gases that surrounds a planet; all the air between the surface of a planet and outer space

carbon dioxide (KAHR-buhn dye-AHK-side): a colorless and odorless gas made from carbon and oxygen

climate (KLYE-mit): the typical weather conditions in a region for at least 30 years

fossil fuels (FAH-suhl FYOO-uhls): nonrenewable resources, such as oil and coal, that come from the remains of ancient plants and animals

glaciers (GLAY-shurz): slow-moving rivers of ice

greenhouse effect (GREEN-hous i-FEKT): the warming of the lower layers of Earth's atmosphere caused by carbon dioxide and other gases that prevent the Sun's heat from escaping

habitat (HAB-i-tat): the natural home or environment of a plant or animal

satellites (SAT-uh-lites): spacecrafts that are sent into orbit around Earth to collect data, transmit information, and perform other functions

weather (WETH-ur): the state of the atmosphere over a very short period of time

INDEX

Arctic 15

carbon 8, 9, 10, 11, 14, 16,
   17, 20, 21

fossil fuels 8, 10

greenhouse 8, 9, 11, 18,
   20, 21

plants 4, 10, 14

polar bears 14

satellite(s) 7, 16, 17

sea levels 4, 5

Sun/Sun's 8, 10, 12

weather 4, 6, 7

AFTER READING QUESTIONS

1. How are weather and climate different?

2. What are some of the effects of climate change?

3. How do scientists know that the climate of Earth is changing?

ABOUT THE AUTHOR

Christina Earley lives in South Florida with her husband, son, and dog. Her favorite subject in school was science. She enjoys learning the science behind the world around her, such as how roller coasters work. She loves mint chocolate chip ice cream and mermaids.

Written by: Christina Earley
Design by: Kathy Walsh
Editor: Kim Thompson

Library of Congress PCN Data
Global Climate Change / Christina Earley
 Earth and Space Science
 ISBN 979-8-8873-5365-4 (hard cover)
 ISBN 979-8-8873-5450-7 (paperback)
 ISBN 979-8-8873-5535-1 (EPUB)
 ISBN 979-8-8873-5620-4 (eBook)
 Library of Congress Control Number: 2023930210

Printed in the United States of America.

Photographs/Shutterstock: Cover & Title pg: sdecoret, KK.KICKIN, Aksenova Nadezhd, amudsenh; p 4-23: amudsenh; p 2, 3, 14, 15: sdecoret, KK.KICKIN; p 5, 9, 11, 13, 15: Hlidskjalf; p 4: NT_Studio; p 5: Bernhard Staehli; p 6: Vadven; p 7: amoun; p 9: Designua, photowind; p 10: BABAROGA; p 11: VectorMine; p 12: buradaki; p 13: seo byeong gon; p 15: Lotus_studio, jo Crebbin; p 16: AleksB59; p 17: Lieutenant Elizabeth Crapo, NOAA Corps, AIRS @Flickr; p 18: I. Noyan Yilmaz; p 19: Stock Unit; p 21: Pixel-Shot, Carlyn Inverson, NOAA.

Seahorse Publishing Company

www.seahorsepub.com

Published in the United States
Seahorse Publishing
PO Box 771325
Coral Springs, FL 33077

SEAHORSE
PUBLISHING